All Souls

All Souls

POEMS

Saskia Hamilton

Graywolf Press

This publication is made possible, in part, by the voters of Minnesota through a Minnesota State Arts Board Operating Support grant, thanks to a legislative appropriation from the arts and cultural heritage fund. Significant support has also been provided by the McKnight Foundation, the Amazon Literary Partnership, and other generous contributions from foundations, corporations, and individuals. To these organizations and individuals we offer our heartfelt thanks.

Published by Graywolf Press
212 Third Avenue North, Suite 485
Minneapolis, Minnesota 55401

www.graywolfpress.org

Published in the United States of America

ISBN 978-1-64445-263-9 (paperback)
ISBN 978-1-64445-264-6 (ebook)

2 4 6 8 9 7 5 3 1
First Graywolf Printing, 2023

Library of Congress Control Number: 2022952324

Cover design: Jeenee Lee

Cover art: Daniel Brush. *Koald 108: Remembrance of Things Present, Seven Days*, 2007. Detail from "Day 2." Ink on paper. 60 x 40 in. (152.4 x 101.6 cm).

For John Justus Lucien Hamilton, always

CONTENTS

Faring   5

Exits and Entrances to the Auditorium   11

All Souls   33

Museum Going   69

Notes   79

Acknowledgments   85

All Souls

FARING

—

Light before you call it light graying the sky. Doves on window ledges call and answer, a low branching into seven-fold division.

'As' means *like* but also means *while*: As a cloud passes. As the shadow in the early morning. As the door turns on the hinge.

Who was it who said that every narrative is a soothing down.

Winter sun floods the table.

—

Quarter past ten: Wave of nausea after morning pills, hot tea, six candles. Thin sheets of cloud now dominant.

The boy wants glow sticks as protection.

Radiator—is it a hiss or a shush? An aspirant or a consolation? Half our days spent living in the future, an illusion.

—

Six days later: as the light grows, so does my will for the weight that tethers us to the ground, shoulder blades descending and meeting.

Flowers at once religious, secular, and sexual.

Blue sky, a dot of cloud. Voices of children from the street below; children with a ball.

Builders are raising the scaffolding, preparing their day's work. Talk with a friend, who was taken by the wolf at night.

——

Sediment on the windows, light flecks the edges of buildings, wind works at the building, worrying it, cyclist with a flickering lamp on the avenue below.

Shadow of a neighbor crosses the window in the building opposite.

——

Strength of feeling now vanished but the memory of it is of a kinship of some kind.

In its recollection, it registers unease beneath the day.

'I love you,' he says, 'but maybe we shouldn't profess our love for one another because, you know, it might mean you'll die?'

—–

And what is actual? The word derives from a cauterizing agent, 'red-hot.' Is actual for one time only, as if only once could something be realized? In its weakened sense, it is 'opposed to potential, possible, ideal.' Beside me on the sofa, the boy is restless with joyous movement and intermittent improvised joy.

—–

In the streets below, each passerby carries time internally, it opens the mind like a flower blown in its native bed.

William Cowper in his laundered kerchief at table. He stares out of the poem in alarm.

—–

By rue d'Amsterdam, inside the rib of the building, crowds rush to three imminent trains, wait by the sandwich and coffee kiosk, trailed by wheeled luggage, pigeons, soldiers moving among them. The eye of the corporal passes over a bystanding neighbor.

Listings and times flap, click, shuffle, the building lists towards departure as if inclined to hear the far-off sound that marks the end of land.

Musical interlude, another train entering the great mouth.

EXITS AND ENTRANCES TO THE AUDITORIUM

—–

'But the history of no life is a jest.' Hallucinatory dream sentence, that, while up in the night again as if I had a newborn, seamlessly integrating into the running sleep narrative of that hour.

Bashō at the end of his life noted the restlessness, the insuppressibility, of thought—

> As for dream, it wanders
> the withered fields.

And what does fear mask? Give it room, ask it a question.

Was it seventy years ago that Kenneth Tynan played the role of Fear in *The Masque of Hope*? ('I mummify transience,' he wrote about the same time.)

According to Kant, we are compelled to bring a form of structuring activity to experience. 'Human reason, in one sphere of its cognition, is called upon to consider questions, which it cannot decline, as they are presented by its own nature, but which it cannot answer, as they transcend every faculty of the mind.' Accordingly, structure of any kind is a form of thought, even counting.

I went to a showing of *The Seventh Seal* at the Paris Theater, on the last Sunday in July. We met on the blinding pavement, Peig and I, then entered the cool dark. I'd forgotten the opening—shrill voices singing something meant to be glorious—then a spoken line from Revelation:

And when the Lamb had opened the seventh seal, there
was silence in heaven about the space of half an hour—

I was interested in the phrase 'about the space of . . . .' Not as a rough
estimate, not approximately or even referring 'to things scattered
over a surface,' but of measurement and circumference 'around the
outside, on every side, all round . . . in every direction.' How com-
forting, to have such precision in the midst of that terror.

Not time and space, but time as space. The space you take up on
earth is a period of time, set by luck or the spinner, the allotter, the
one with scissors.

One might pray not to be at the mercy of the mind's wanderings
in the final hour. What about the unraveling of thought, the de-
structuring of mind?

Bound in blankets for half an hour in the long cigar tube of the
PET scan machine, there is no clock to agree to, to find comfort in.
Instructed to lie still, unable to clear my throat, I tried to suppress
the mind's hallucinatory lurid wanderings by going through the son-
nets but always lost my way at the seventh or eighth line,

and then I tried to hear songs, to reconstruct the lyrics, to divide up
the time, or even to hum in order

to hear the sound of 'inseparate words' in my chest.

Then I began to count, to twenty, to make the length between one
and two, and two and three, and three and four, long enough so that
at twenty I would be quarter-inched backwards through the machine

a stop, time passing more slowly from numeral to numeral, to fill the space of half an hour

—because if the count went past twenty it would be somehow unbearable—because immeasurable.

That breathing continues (if we continue) is hidden in the meaning of words we have for inaudible pauses and endings—the French *un temps*, a time, or the English *period*, full stop or duration.

Silence and breaths taken punctuate our speaking. Rests indicate the pace of the movement of thought; they are instructions for listening.

—–

In the old photograph, the group of seven children (c. 1875?) peer at the camera as if it could not be trusted to stand still, they bend towards it like tulips with minds of their own. One of them, Henry, leans past his book to say something. He was the one who ended his life in Italy among the lemon trees, but as a boy his gaze is warm and direct, as if all would want to forgive him any transgression he might with his good nature mistakenly take in the course of his foreshortened life—

I would like to hear more of that.

Anton, who died of syphilis, his arm too long for his jacket sleeve

Jo the jurist, Betsy, Clara's dry wit about the eyes

Lex with the toy boat who would study the setting of the winds, too fluid for structural composition—

My aim was to calm the imagination not to excite it. But I could not utter the word *curiosity*. My breath failed the four times I punctuated my sentence with the word.

—‑

To listen to our own breathing and to someone else's is to experience someone's else: an intimate sameness (if we are in accord); an else-ness, if not. Patterns of breathing are both involuntary—the breath of deep sleep, of hard labor—and interpretive. Changes in the rhythm of inhalation and exhalation register emotion, the rising emotions of anticipation, fear, anxiety, and excitement, and the easing emotions, recovery from heightened states, being relieved in mind, being in one's element.

——

Dickinson's words and graphic marks describe the movement of late afternoon light:

> When it comes, the Landscape listens –
> Shadows – hold their breath –
> When it goes, 'tis like the Distance
> On the look of Death –

The dashes induce shortness of breath in the reader, as if we are meant to mimic the shadows in their intent listening. We pause to hear a sound so faint it may only be visible.

What do the landscape's shadows anticipate? For when the light passes, their edges will be erased, they will vanish. Or will they have complete dominion?

The boy darts through the room rustling and clicking, his YouTubers screaming distortions into the microphone and shouting at the zombies killing their avatars.

Is the clicking the sound of a plastic tray of cookies or a toy I forgot we had?

The volume is turned low enough.

Outside, bursts of jackhammers—smaller implosions of the same along with the starting and stopping air conditioners. Late August, sudden cooling.

—-

'Come sleep! O sleep, the certain knot of peace,' Sidney wrote. And so forth.

In the papers, we read in the shorthand *A.N.D.* permission to allow natural death. So the day continues. Meanwhile, the ill among us are everywhere—swimming in their clothes, all ages, overdressed, making efforts at elegance despite a loss of appetite for all appetitive things except the easing of pain. They remind me of myself, one of them now, marking time, using the word *hope* in familiar phrases, using conjunctions and all to be taken side by side with, along with, that which precedes it, loving the forgetful ease in the bodily well all around.

—-

Adult to child, 'Do you think I'm good at telling the difference between a truth and a lie?'

Yes.

'What are you good at?'

I'm good at existing.

—–—

In *Not I*, the mouth is the only thing visible in the entire theater, except for a mysterious 'dead still' Auditor, who punctuates the mouth's speech with a 'raising of arms from sides and their falling back, in a gesture of helpless compassion.'

Billie Whitelaw recalled Beckett directing her in the play:

> He was so demanding in as much that he was so meticulous. If you said an 'oh' instead of an 'ah' or an 'and' instead of something else, you know, from the stalls you'd hear 'oh lord,' or see his head going down into his hands.

And there is Beckett's play *Breath*, which, after a 'Faint brief cry and immediately inspiration and slow increase of light,' lasts thirty-five seconds and has no words.

——

Although the remedy does not exist, the remedy is no exit, only death is—

there was the time a friend brought the Prince of Denmark to the door and she gave him a cup of chocolate amongst the Kokoschka and Dix and Grosz and Beckmann prints that hung in the room of chintz and old furniture like the soul itself, collective soul of suffering, peering from behind the arras into the curious gallery of polite forgetful living space, with three windows and two doors.

— —

In the dying, breath changes, coming very quickly at a certain passage—it seems a panic—and then calms, slowing immensely as the pauses between grow longer. Those keeping vigil can miss when the last has occurred. Donne noticed this:

> As virtuous men passe mildly away,
>   And whisper to their soules, to goe,
> Whilst some of their sad friends doe say,
>   The breath goes now, and some say, no:

Is the light gone out of someone's eyes unmistakable, like late-afternoon light suddenly dropping?

> If I an ordinary nothing were,
> As shadow, a light, and body must be here.

'But I am none,' Donne says.

—–

Moonlight, 'most amazing of roses,' gone now, uprooted, though the Stanwell Perpetual, derived from the *Rosa spinosissima*, still stands. The roses in memory only now—deadheading, wear gloves for the thorns, aborted branches, that radiate from the stems. Do not be timid with the shears.

Raising a child not a reader. Readers are scattered in families like wildflower seeds. One or two in a generation.

Can writing be a form of practice or of preparation for death?

All that the mind visualizes—rolled stockings, evening clothes, co-lostomy bags, Mademoiselle Godiva, *The Vanishing*, the vanquished, parable of the sower, the high street and the *loup pendu* crossing, spangled lace and gorgeous concoctions, Vigée Le Brun, concord, forms of cruelty, besotted adjectives, tertiary syphilis and public enemies, centers for the humanities, centers for the study of war, center or middle point of something, surgically repositioned navels—is a threat, a destabilization, in the moment of confrontation.

The imprisoned poet was forbidden pencil, paper, and all books save the Bible. He composed during that time by wetting the tip of his finger and running it over a word on the scritta paper. He thought of rolling cigarettes, licking them closed, assembled the poems from his collection of raised words. Wisps of smoke.

Take a deep breath. They will run out.

Whitman's breath is long and open; he is restless with death.

> I have heard what the talkers were talking . . . . the talk of
> the beginning and the end,
> But I do not talk of the beginning or the end.

His invitations to the reader are generous, lonely.

> Stop this day and night with me and you shall possess the
> origin of all poems.

When thoughts are left without a body to animate them, marks on the paper indicate someone was here. *Here* is the place where two kinds of time intersect, moments successive and moments infinite.

The Dutch word for pause or suspension is *onderbreking*, a disturbance within the order of moments.

Sounds of the household in other rooms while one drifts in and out of sleep, the care of friends, the duration of a day of illness in the space of half an hour.

Jam cooking in a saucepan.

People faced death yesterday for thousands of years, it's true!

The entombed scrolls of the Egyptian *Book of the Dead* were originally called the *Book of Coming Forth by Day*, and the Tibetan one combines two texts also called *The Great Liberation through Hearing*.

You can tell the dead from the living in the old poems by their surprise at the guides. Where they're heading, no guides, just a crowd gathered at the shore, where it's quiet.

One of us hums to hear inseparate words resounding in the sternum.

——

Early afternoon snow falling on the city. From the chemotherapy suites, lights coming on in the offices of the building opposite.

What would Dan Flavin make of stained ceiling tiles and the semi-circular industrial lights here and in the Integrative Medicine Center of the cancer hospital? Some forms of symmetry—

As for man, his days are as grass . . .

For the wind passeth over it, and it is gone.

Drops hanging from the wrought iron window guards, white sky, wet brick and sandstone. Soaked water towers.

Vagary—wandering or devious journey, a roaming about or abroad.

So is the final confrontation, with the mind spinning.

Age of grievance and complaint.

Back at home, the boy chattering, speaking to his game.

What is the veil that writing and description put over all things? Narrative, scene, setting, persuasion . . .

And then there is Antinous as Osiris, lord of silence, transformed by Hadrian in his grief.

What practice will help prepare me.

Reading Zbigniew Herbert writing to Ryszard Krynicki on the black foam of the newspapers, urns of ashes in the burned garden, owl's puzzles in the night.

We wake from sleep to sleep—the radiator knocking the floorboard, the dead poet and the elderly poet rowing us into the night, second sleep coming.

While those emperors of speed, the swifts, stir in the south and make their way, sleeping above us in the air.

ALL SOULS

––

In the cupboard, a pocket watch in its case,
velvet ribbon knotted on the click and winder
black as wet roads, soft as a tongue
in the shadow of a closed mouth.
Its precision jewel bearing is ruby.
Its spade and whip hands would snap off with pressure
from the smallest finger. And yet
the escapement enforces its circle
of unbreakable numbers. Someone
has let it run down. Don't turn back,
it's the wrong way, is the relation of
chronology to history at all valuable here.

—-—

Chemical burring of the tongue.
Good to be on the other side
of treatment for now.

We scroll on. Would a codex restore
the balance of recto and verso.

Take up the book. Dreams luminous
in anticipation of the alarm.
When it comes, how dark and modest waking is.

——

There are five mobs chasing the PPK Gamer,
the boy has a bow and spins in the air.

—‒

7:20, the school bus just gone.
The driver swung the doors shut
and the faces of the children pressed
to the windows as it drove off
towards the river.

—-—

Late in the season, eating a pear
that is the memory of a pear,

silvery, dunked in frigid waters
by the orchard keepers for transport,
mealy now, late season, fragrant
of September and sun.

I was in the dictionary looking up
the distinction between necessity
and need, or requirement, 'the constraining
power of circumstances.' The dictionary
gives examples from Sidney and Golding:
Of the necessitie that is conditionall,
and not of the necessitie that is
absolute. Sidney met his end one morning
when, writes Greville, by the banks of the IJssel,
an 'unfortunate hand' sent forth a bullet
that broke the bone in his thigh.
So great was his thirst, he asked
for drink; but before it touched his lips,
he saw a 'poor soldier carried along'
who 'ghastly cast his eyes up' at the bottle.
Sidney gave it to him. You, whose
'necessity,' he said, 'is yet greater than mine.'
Within weeks, and with the 'fixing
of a lover's thought on those eternal
beauties,' he died in Arnhem on the baker's street.

—–

She passed all along a room a bottle
of currant juice, it went 'from hand to hand
along all the stretchers,' she wrote,
some twenty-five or more, and came back
'still half-full.' Someone helped his neighbor
to drink, since he had 'no hands.'
The battle of Arnhem—and pressed in her house
by the river there lay three hundred
or more, one doctor, one orderly.
The children sheltered in the cellar. She
attended the men, read the English psalms
to them, 'Surely he shall deliver thee
from the snare of the fowler,' she read,
'He shall cover thee with his feathers,
and under his wings shalt thou trust.'
She returned to the cellar.
'What a long time you have been away,'
her daughter said, and asked for her doll's
white linen. Again she climbed the stairs
and at the top she found 'a whole piece
of the wall under the window . . .
blown away,' the wounded with it.

—–

Thaon

Between the fields, the asphalt velvety
in the rain. Where is the road bending to
beyond? Green everywhere on the ground,
though it's still the season of sleep.
Sleep after harrowing, refinement,
after dispersal.

—–

Out of the window of the Committee
on Preschool Special Education,
a triangular intersection
of traffic at the uptown crossing.
The parents, here without their children,
to petition on their behalf, are lonely
only in this passageway, the unaccompanied
shelter of the twelfth floor where they are signed in
by a kindly woman to spend some hours
waiting for a supervisor always
late with the correspondent gates of paperwork
but who has primary authority to accede
or deny in many languages, for
there is no loneliness in the company
of children. With an air of apology,
the young woman calls out *Miss, Sir,*
not knowing the names, and they try to catch
in her glance to whom she wishes to speak,
but the optic axes of her eyes
coincide divergently, catching
two families simultaneously, every face
responds with apology to the summons,
the clerk's oblique eyes calling each of them,
none of them, all of them, generally beheld.

—-

Is there point to critical interpretation
that gives us 'what we all know already, what
inescapably and instantly strikes
the eye,' as Rosen wrote in the summer issue?
Then Ricks asked if Rosen would agree
to any like assertion of a musical phrase
striking the ear? I spent the hours that season
in a basement library magnifying
Bishop's hand ten times to read the word
'tidal.' On the daily train along
the river, the conductor sometimes returned,
sometimes pocketed, my ticket.
'An interpretation,' Rosen said,
'must either uncover or create a secret.'
'I give you simply what you have already,'
reasoned Lowell. A fine morning.
Steady summer construction
on the avenue stories below.

— —

After the peace, November Sunday,
a fine one, smallest child inside, eldest
on a train journey, and he and a friend
in the apple orchard by the river.
He wore the military duty belt,
the find from the brush that he'd been snapped in
a few days before. They found the tree to climb
and then jumped down this time
onto a mine that had once—though the field
had been swept, they all thought—been laid there
by an unfortunate hand. For sixty years,
his face looks up from picture frames
in the houses of their friends. She kept
in her clothes a piece of his skull,
and her thumb would stroke it,
as she had once stroked the fontanel.

—–

'He has an ethic of solidarity with the victims
of history,' Heaney said of Herbert. He wanted
his vast book of collected poems to be 'open
to everyone in the world.' And 'to hold the line.'

The Archangel also 'had forewarned
Adam, by dire example, to beware.'
This afternoon, at the Neue Galerie,
Franz Marc, *Die ersten Tiere* (1913)—one turns

this way on the way to the field.
Felix Nussbaum's memories of crowds
and gatherings (1925), where
does that line lead, what are they pressing

to see, their backs to us? Will we join them?
Knowing comes later, later may be
aftermath, or prelude. An introductory
statement is stenciled on the gallery wall.

Bonjour Tristesse on the Penguin Classics
mug. Which recollects the friend at the bar
who kept saying '*bonjour, Tristesse*' to an
exasperated stranger, over and over,
as was their subsequent, brief affair,
they'd meet before seven, it was at
an end for good each time. Goodness came along

later, in the form of you, your 'aquiline
profile,' as Ms. Hardwick remarked
when she saw the photograph taken
with my last good camera, my own brief story
of tea in the cup with the figure
of the arctic bird from the London zoo
we went to that first Sunday, you who lived near

the zoos of Paris, Dublin, Amsterdam,
to rise to the sounds of creatures
calling for breakfast from the keepers,
so triste and wonder pale we were,
from each our own pasts, burnt as we had been
by the mere rising of the sun,
the good days ahead, the winter gifts

yet to be gifted. One day.

—–

New Year's drizzle, nine, every church in the City
solitary. Empty roads, bus gone.
We stood on the curb looking at
Hawksmoor's façade. The churchyard dead
were removed for the coming of the Underground.
Does it help to remember them
when hearing the sound of time?
Inside, in the long and narrow, pleas
for intercession on yellow post-its
left by the candles. A plaque for John Newton
and other former reverends unknown.

— —

Half a street away, he slung a bag
on his shoulder and walked down rue Delambre
past Raspail and the street sweeper,
wet pavement. Dawn. One city
becomes two, constitutive
as against incidental, dividing
within the structure as cells divide.

—

Achterhoek

The sky clay-white, ashen—'ash not a dirty
but a clean thing' J. Ryle once said.
Inside, cool sinks

to the corners, the flagstone convergence
of floor and walls where children sometimes
leave a treasure,

and up in the rafters wattle insulation,
paint cans, gas bottles, oxidized blades
of old implements oily with dust,

always there above the games, meals, foot
traffic, summer parties, who and what
moves across and beneath time.

Day's end. Labor easing though not the rain.
'The elements are triumphing,'
says Ryle. Indoors then from 'the old, gray city,'
or was it the sullen streets, passing
the hall to the room, lamplit, dry,
the voice of O., my grandmother, in memory,
from memory, reading the Victorian pages
of the book, entries marked with pencil:
'My task accomplish'd and the long day done,
My wages taken . . .'

—–

She is dying, said the nurse. It was a Tuesday
in the new century. But not then—
she found strength again, her sturdy legs
kept their footing in the beige laced shoes.
A greenwood of beeches outside her window.
A Wednesday, Thursday, Friday.
A Saturday. A Sunday.

—-—

Schubert, Schumann said, wrote music as if
'never in doubt as to how to continue,'
but his notes, conversant with the seemly structure of
thinking, accommodated the stops, the rests, interlude,
word inserted to prevent hiatus,
an opening, an aperture, a break in continuity
                              —an early death,
not much time, he could persuade the line
of thought to bend this way and bring it to belief.

––

In search of a medicinal hour. Hortus:
sitting at the café with apple cake
while garden goers stir the gravel path.
Compacted here, luxuriant trained growth
of teaberry, gentian, trumpet vine,
comfrey, field restharrow, &c.
Our apothecary ancestor with his *liber ingressus*
token entered here to gather the herbs
for infusions that were to aid the unwell
caught in the far gone far alone glance
of mortality, moving the clock hands
from one hour into the hour.
Who is there now to announce the triumph
of hope? But by and by, after
seeds have been scattered, stirred and covered over,
blossomed, gathered, dried, crushed. Hot, late afternoon,
bees crossing bees and white butterflies.

—–

Amsterdam → Zutphen

Late departure, hot carriage slowing
just minutes out of the station.
The book opens to June 1797,
Wordsworth and Coleridge meet again,
1798, travel together,
W. homesick, C. to Göttingen.
Beechwood below, grass, fern, brambles.
W. 'felt more invested in memory
than philosophy.' Rows of mown fields.
Now and again, at speed, life at rest—
train drivers chatting, small child on a giant bench,
distorted clanging at the crossings,
two horses, a donkey, the first animals,
then open landscape, nature 'a realm
of intuitions and affections,'
interrupted by discharged soldiers, the dead,
all that was cut down hanging still in the scent,
leaving the west for the east, O. in decline,
stricken and anxious alders, aren't we all,
copse of birch, then mostly beech.

In the chained library in Zutphen,
the Old Testament was bound for the fathers
by a bookbinder who stamped images
of Luther inside the leather covers;
he was employed for a year before they caught
on, 1575–76. Ten years later, in September,
the siege. Why today is it empty in the town,
glossy fruit in tiers outside the grocers,
plump red currants, gooseberries,
blackberries in small green cartons,
no sign of Philip Sidney, only beyond
the walls, in the grass by the river.

—-

'Death closes all.' Yes. But were they granted
anything, none know beforehand,
breath going out for a decade,
returning in a century,
while those gathered there fall out of
their own pockets, or is it
the count and rhythm, unable
to fix a mark or a lover's thought
at the moment when the face of the encounter
became knowledge completed.

Home from school. From the other room, the washer
revolving. And the child playing virtually
with a friend: 'I'm going to duplicate
my optic staff.'

——

The church in the valley is abandoned now,
mold climbing the stone walls,
soft mud in the mire, clusters of gentian
and sword grass by the footpath.

Holy holy sang its choristers,
the generations of children of
children of children of children over
a thousand years. Speak, tongue.

And 'the swallows interweaving' there,
Coleridge noted sometime between
1794 and 1798.

Reading the news, waiting for sleep or the night to pass, tap of rain on the window unit, desk of unfinished work in the next room. X the painter has died. Images in my hand of the enormous faces she painted, the cause of death in narrative paragraphs, all the world of representation compressed on the screen.

Why retell the stories of those before us? They already spoke them, or held their tongues—fell silent. A lifetime to overcome the prohibition not to. But the lens is all wrong these days. I'd thought it a sunset, a sketch, told again as all sunsets are. To say something sincerely yet inauthentically is the danger. And Eliot struck 'Ode' from the first US edition of his poems to prevent his mother from seeing it . . .

What prompted that thought? Body does not want to sit up just yet. One two one two go the taps. The child stirs—light herewith emitted in the dark.

—-

How strange—but then '*strange* should be dried out
for a millennium,' Ricks says. *Journey,*
too. Poor old words. Even so, how *out
of the way - ?* to be the subject.
To whom would it be otherwise?
Who becomes familiar with mortal
illness for very long. I was a stranger, &c.
Not everyone appreciates it, no
one finds being the third person
becoming, it's never accurate,
and then one is headed for the past tense.
Futurity that was once a lark, a gamble,
a chance messenger, traffic and trade, under sail.
The boy touches your arm in his sleep
for ballast. It's warm in the hold. Between
ship and sky, the bounds of sight
alone, sphere so bounded.

—

Alone in the mountains one day
she felt, she heard, a half-step behind her,
someone, who, the multitude, a sole
companion? Joining her at the left turn
of the road, and she did not break
her stride, her grandson from years hence,
or was it her dead brother from years past,
from childhood, from infancy,
keeping her company for now.

——

At a distance, a small wood islanded
in the meadows. Paths innumerable
through beech and growth, ferns and decay,
shifting light raising the dry scent of
summer sun from the ground.

The quarter-hour abided, it had no
cessation while I stood there astride
the bicycle—what is not bounded
by the limits of perception but looks on,
a door unlatched, ajar—restless
irregular light and shadow, awakened,
having arrived at a turn—

then pushing off. At play with instability,
worthy of mastery, tires going at speed
along the packed sand of a road that ran
from field to field without discernible end
in all of Europe.

— —

Zutphen → Winterswijk

Hot local, this old route I once took each summer
to be met by a brisk smiling someone,
my pale yellow ticket a *liber ingressus*.
The station was a composition with
yellow, iron black, white and gray.
Sometimes I too would go to meet that train,
Opapa, back from France, stepped down with care
from a burgundy car in the evening.

Sometimes I too would go to meet that train,
Opapa, back from France, stepped down with care
from a burgundy car in the evening.

The crow took a cracker and my grandfather
scolded it. Six, drinks under the apple tree,
the foxgloves leaning over flower beds
and down at children sipping juice,
white butterflies among the buddleia
and nettles with their feathery trichomes,
and hover flies in the last uncleared area
where meadow met the garden and lawn, arbor
and house. *Amice* was the crow's name, it stepped
sideways, crossed its beak on the bench.
The order of six o'clock: shoulder blades
settling down the back, salt on fingers,
prints on glasses, books closed, their linen covers
warming in the westerly light.

—–

The child moved through the hour
from fridge to table to fridge again
with sure command, small strength and purpose,
all his might against the magnetic
door gasket. Consented to being dressed,
consented to the descent of stairs,
step over step, to meet the bus,
moving torso, hips, this way and that
in an early dance to the tune
of protest, clutching a black train as he boarded
and the driver swung the doors shut
and I waved at the children pressing their faces
to the windows as it drove towards the river.
May they all be covered by feathers.

MUSEUM GOING

—–

At the end of summer came the visits to the Kröller-Müller, the Mauritshuis, and the Rijksmuseum, with our mother and her family. My brother and I had spent the summer away from her as she had spent the year away from them. The timing lent these visits a ritual quality of reunion and impending departure. The galleries and grounds were quiet, solemn, mostly empty. In the Hoge Veluwe, we drove past miles of heather, and in the gardens paused on damp grass before Bourdelle's sculpture of *La grande Pénélope*.

—–

In The Hague, there again were the faces of the Rembrandts—those gathered for *The Anatomy Lesson* on the second floor by the stairs looked in every direction, and in the lonely portrait of two friends, the eyes of one were cast down. In the next room, in the familiar darkness, the red earth of *Saul and David* (its attribution then in doubt), the king covered his face.

Two Vermeers and a small chained *Goldfinch* of Fabritius hung in a room with silk paneling. Our mother told us to stand anywhere in the gallery and the eyes of the young woman with the earring would find us. The morning sun in the *View of Delft* lit up the eastern side of the city and the church spire where Willem de Zwijger lay buried, tiny beads of lead white on ultramarine, rose madder, and ochre. The sky huge with clouds presaging rain, or reporting its departure.

Light streaming into the gallery and reflecting off the varnish obscured the paintings. When my grandfather leaned on his cane, the floor would give a little. He turned to look from one to another.

——

In the lamplit interior galleries in Amsterdam, milk poured without end into the bowl in Vermeer's *The Milkmaid*.

I didn't give thought to the color of her blue apron until years later. Nor to the blue dress in the painting of a *Woman Reading a Letter*. The two scenes are as if glimpsed, neither the women nor the compositions seem conscious of allegory, except perhaps in the abstract sense of life itself. One is arrested by the poise—a reader in receipt of a message, unassuming in her station and silence. Tomas Tranströmer writes that she is 'in her eighth month'; Robert Lowell that she is 'solid with yearning.'

——

In Proust, Charles Swann sees a pregnant kitchen maid who moves about as with 'an ordinary, rather heavy burden' 'enlarged by the additional symbol which she carried before her, without appearing to understand its meaning.' He calls her 'Giotto's Charity,' a reproduction of which hangs in the summer schoolroom. It is Swann's special nature and his sense of the fluidity of time to think of a fourteenth-century painting as populated with the living.

The maid in Combray retains her independence from, yet is transformed by, proximity to the abstract. Proust again:

> But in later years I came to understand that the arresting strangeness, the special beauty of these frescoes derived from the great part played in them by symbolism, and the fact that this was represented not as a symbol (for the thought symbolised was nowhere expressed) but as a reality, actually felt or materially handled, added something more precise and more literal to the meaning of the work, something more concrete and more striking to the lesson it imparted. Similarly, in the case of the poor kitchen-maid, was not one's attention incessantly drawn to her belly by the weight which dragged it down . . .

I had the sensation, upon reading again of the pregnant young woman, of discovering the very structure of my thinking about the letter-reader in Vermeer. If her dress signals anything, there is nevertheless 'something more concrete and more striking to the lesson' imparted, and the painting does this so successfully that one could look at it without ever thinking of the annunciation, a thought perhaps symbolized but nowhere expressed except in the color blue.

In a passage about orders of design in drama, T. S. Eliot writes of a 'pattern behind the pattern into which the characters deliberately involve themselves; the kind of pattern which we perceive in our own lives only at rare moments of inattention and detachment, drowsing in sunlight. It is the pattern drawn by what the ancient world called Fate.'

Swann's Way was given to me one summer by Huib Drion, a family friend. He promised the other volumes if I caught on. A jurist of distinction and sometime literary essayist. Once, prompted by a friend in her eighties who wished for a way to end her suffering and dependence without violence (leaping before a train, hanging herself), he wrote about the need for a suicide pill for the elderly.

—-

In the sitting room, Drion would fold himself up with a book, drum his fingers on the arm of the sofa, hum an air, spring up and disappear, reappear with another volume. His voice began in a note of high excitement quickly suppressed, as if to say to his own intellectual excitement, 'there there, such nonsense.'

He said about himself as a law student at Leiden that he was 'the most obscure [*obscuur*] student you could possibly imagine.' That is, he wasn't much given to the culture of student societies with their drinking and bullshit.

The word 'obscure' in Dutch, English, French, &c., comes from the Latin, from ob- for 'against' or 'in the way of' the sky. But it is unimaginable to think of him as indiscernible, for in the very quickness of his presence he was always on the point of visible thought, wielding a cane through the ferns on an overcast afternoon walk. When the postman's van reversed down the drive on wet mornings, he gallantly retrieved the mail from the letterbox for my grandmother, handing over the bundle of newspapers, envelopes, postcards. On Mondays, the paper was the *TLS*—she would promptly return it to him in its wrapper, for the pleasure of reading it first. She called him Our Mutual Friend.

——

Last year, I found the first uniform edition of Proust in English, twelve volumes that opened easily to the hand. They were published by Chatto in 1941 during the Blitz—when bookseller WHSmith advertised its wares: 'blacked-out evenings, take home some books'— and sold well enough for a 1943 reprint, despite the constraints of paper rationing.

Drion and his brother created a student newspaper during the war. The first mimeograph of eighty copies of *De Geus onder studenten* was dated 4 October 1940. In November 1940, the university—deemed a *horzelnest* (hornet's nest)—was closed. They published as the brothers 'De Jong,' distant enough in pronunciation to 'Drion' to obscure the connection. Their lives may have been spared in part by this hiding by mishearing. If the doorbell rang, they put the typewriter and the mimeograph machine under the floorboards. He spoke with high tension of distributing the papers to letterboxes by bicycle. In 1943 a flyer making the rounds stated that the 'De Jong' brothers were wanted by the Sicherheitsdienst. 'It is actually a miracle that we were never arrested,' Drion said. They taped cyanide pills to their ankles in case of such an eventuality.

He told the story of Han Gelder, 'a young man, barely in his twenties, whom I greatly admired and who had managed to unite the resistance at all the Dutch universities—he had ensured that *De Geus* was printed and distributed throughout.' Gelder was caught in an SD raid on an illegal printer's shop on January 21, 1944: 'He always carried a gun with him because he was afraid he would not be able to withstand torture. During the raid, he pulled his gun and shot a German officer and then himself.' Gelder's colleague and co-conspirator, Wim Eggink, arrested the same night, died under torture a year later.

De Geus ran for thirty issues, through 13 July 1945, with a final print run of 5,000.

— —

In his first essay on Proust, Drion wrote that the novel captured 'the solitariness and inexpressibility of human lives (the *'solitude morale'* of the Romantic).' The loneliness of that theme running alongside the 'unbelievable richness of orchestration' [*ongelofelijke rijkdom van de 'orkestratie'*] was his idea of its greatness.

He particularly admired Proust's writing about the *View of Delft*, which he praised for being as 'poetic and lucid' as the painting.

In *La Prisonnière*, Proust's Bergotte reads a review in the newspaper about the *View of Delft*, a painting possessing 'a beauty that was sufficient in itself' [*d'une beauté qui se suffirait à elle-même*]. Then 'ate a few potatoes, left the house, and went to the exhibition' [*mangea quelques pommes de terre, sortit et entra à l'exposition*]. Bergotte weighed his life's work against a detail in the painting and found his wanting, in its imperfections. Indigestion, the sting of death, collapses him.

— —

From Swann's vision of the pregnant young woman, the narrator turns his mind to the end of life:

> Similarly, in the case of the poor kitchen-maid, was not one's attention incessantly drawn to her belly by the weight which dragged it down; and in the same way, again, are not the thoughts of the dying often turned towards the practical, painful, obscure, visceral aspect, towards that 'seamy side' of death [*vers cet envers de la mort*] which is, as it happens, the side that death actually presents to them and forces them to feel, a side which far more closely resembles a crushing burden, a difficulty in breathing, a destroying thirst, than the abstract idea to which we are accustomed to give the name of Death [*l'idée de la mort*]?

Scott Moncrieff translates '*cet envers*' as the 'seamy side,' which brings with its materiality a connotation of aversion and shame. Proust looks more plainly on the body giving way to 'a crushing burden, a difficulty in breathing, a destroying thirst.' In her translation, Lydia Davis opts for 'the underside of death.'

It was the rational wish to alleviate the suffering of those imprisoned by age and illness that turned Drion's mind as a legal scholar towards a pill that would permit a consent to death, unaccompanied—he was an atheist—by any moral or religious opprobrium.

——

Drion would accompany us sometimes to the museums. In truth, with the visits to the galleries and grounds comes a memory of longueur and hunger, since we were young children. In the Hoge Veluwe, the adults paused at and praised the monumental patience in Bourdelle's *La grande Pénélope*, the foreboding they saw in bronze cast just before the Great War.

Afterwards we ate pannekoeken in the sun and shifting clouds. Drion was a gentle remover of what Proust called '*furieux et légers*' ('*razend en licht*,' 'frenzied and light') wasps on the wing near the jam.

NOTES

Faring

'Man in society is like a flower / Blown in its native bed,' William Cowper, *The Task, Book IV: The Winter Evening* (1785).

Exits and Entrances to the Auditorium

'But the history of no life is a jest': Louise Brooks, in Kenneth Tynan, 'The Girl in the Black Helmet: Louise Brooks,' *Show People: Profiles in Entertainment* (1979), 273.

'As for dream . . .': see Robert Hass, 'Images,' *Twentieth-Century Pleasures* (1987), 276–278, and *The Essential Haiku* (1994).

'I mummify transience': Kenneth Tynan, *He That Plays the King: A View of the Theatre* (1950), 252.

'Human reason, in one sphere . . .': Immanuel Kant, *The Critique of Pure Reason* (1781), tr. J. M. D. Meiklejohn.

'And when the Lamb . . .': *The Seventh Seal*, dir. Ingmar Bergman (1957).

'Inseparate words': Algernon Charles Swinburne, *Atalanta in Calydon* (1865).

'Someone's else': from Christopher Ricks, who attributes it to T. S. Eliot.

'When it comes, the Landscape listens . . .': Emily Dickinson, '[There's a certain Slant of light]' #320, *The Poems of Emily Dickinson*, ed. Ralph W. Franklin (1999).

'Come, sleep! O sleep': Sir Philip Sidney, *Astrophil and Stella* 39 (c. 1582).

'He was so demanding . . .': Billie Whitelaw, *A Wake for Sam* (BBC, 1990).

'As virtuous men passe mildly away . . .': John Donne, 'A Valediction: Forbidding Mourning' (1633).

'If I an ordinary nothing were . . .': John Donne, 'A Nocturnal upon St. Lucy's Day' (1633).

'Most amazing of roses': from a rose catalogue.

'I have heard . . .' and 'Stop this day and night . . .': Walt Whitman, *Song of Myself* (1855).

'The entombed scrolls . . .': see Ptolemy Tompkins, *The Modern Book of the Dead* (2012).

'As for man . . .': Psalm 103.

'Black foam . . .': Zbigniew Herbert, 'To Ryszard Krynicki—a Letter,' *Report from the Besieged City*, tr. John and Bogdana Carpenter (1985), with thanks to Peter Sacks.

All Souls

I was in the dictionary: '*Of the necessitie* . . .': 'necessity,' *OED2* (1989). 'Unfortunate hand . . .': Fulke Greville, *A Dedication to Sir Philip Sidney* (c. 1610–1612); reprinted as *The Life of the Renowned Sir Philip Sidney* (1652).

She passed all along a room a bottle: See K. A. ter Horst-Arriëns, *A Regimental Aid Post of the 1st British Airborne Division at Oosterbeek, September 17–26, 1944.* 'Surely he shall deliver thee . . .': Psalm 91.

Is there point to critical interpretation: 'what we all know already . . .': Charles Rosen, 'The Revelations of Frank Kermode,' *The New York Review of Books* (9 June 2011). Elizabeth Bishop's papers are in the Vassar College Library. 'I give you simply': Robert Lowell, 'The Vanity of Human Wishes,' *Near the Ocean* (1967).

He has an ethic of solidarity: Seamus Heaney, 'The Poetry of Zbigniew Herbert' (Irish Writers' Centre, 16 October 2008). 'Had forewarned / Adam': John Milton, *Paradise Lost*, VII 41–42. 'memories of crowds': see Felix Nussbaum, *Remembering Grüßau* and *Fairground* (both 1925).

Bonjour Tristesse: Françoise Sagan, *Bonjour Tristesse* (1954). 'triste / and wonder pale': John Lydgate *Siege of Thebes* (c. 1420–1422).

Day's end. Labor easing. 'the old, gray city' and 'My task accomplish'd . . .': W. E. Henley, 'Margaritae Sorori' (1886). 'Sullen streets . . .': see Elizabeth Hardwick to Robert Lowell, 3 June 1973, and footnote, *The Dolphin Letters: Elizabeth Hardwick, Robert Lowell, and Their Circle* (2019), 346.

Schubert, Schumann said: Robert Schumann on Franz Schubert's final three sonatas.

In search of a medicinal hour: Hortus Botanicus, botanical garden in Amsterdam.

Late departure, hot carriage slowing: 'a realm of intuitions and affections': see Ralph Pite, 'Wordsworth and the Natural World,' *The Cambridge Companion to William Wordsworth* (2003).

'Death closes all': Alfred, Lord Tennyson, 'Ulysses' (1842).

The church in the valley: 'Speak, tongue' (*loqui lingua*) adapted from St. Thomas Aquinas, *'Pange Lingua'* (c. 1263). For Coleridge's swallows, see *Coleridge's Notebooks: A Selection*, ed. Seamus Perry (2002), 31.

Reading the news: 'Eliot struck': see *The Poems of T. S. Eliot*, ed. Christopher Ricks and Jim McCue (2015), v. I, 1177.

Museum Going

Dedicated to Elise Wiarda.

Tomas Tranströmer: 'Vermeer,' tr. Samuel Charters, in *Selected Poems, 1954–1986*, edited by Robert Hass (1987).

Robert Lowell: 'Epilogue,' *Day by Day* (1977).

'An ordinary, rather heavy burden . . .': Marcel Proust, *Remembrance of Things Past*, tr. C. K. Scott Moncrieff and Terence Kilmartin (1983), vol 1, 87.

'But in later years . . .': Marcel Proust, *Remembrance of Things Past*, tr. C. K. Scott Moncrieff and Terence Kilmartin (1983), vol 1, 88.

'Pattern behind the pattern . . .': T. S. Eliot, *Elizabethan Essays* (1934), 194.

Hornet's nest: see Robert van Genechten, *Het Horzelnest* (2019).

'The solitariness and inexpressibility . . .': Huib Drion, *Het conservative hart en andere essays* (1966), 106.

'Poetic and lucid': Huib Drion, *Het conservatieve hart en andere essays* (1966), 99.

'A beauty . . .': Marcel Proust, *Remembrance of Things Past*, tr. C. K. Scott Moncrieff and Terence Kilmartin (1983), vol 3, 185.

'*D'une beauté* . . .': Marcel Proust, *La Prisonnière, vol 3, A la recherche du temps perdu*, ed. and annotated by Pierre Clarac and André Ferré (1969), 186–87.

'Similarly, in the case of the poor kitchen-maid': Marcel Proust, *Remembrance of Things Past*, tr. C. K. Scott Moncrieff and Terence Kilmartin (1983), vol 1, 88; *A la recherche du temps perdu*, ed. and annotated by Pierre Clarac and André Ferré (1969), vol 1, 82.

'Underside of death': Marcel Proust, *The Way by Swann's*, vol. 1 of *In Search of Lost Time*, tr. and with an introduction and notes by Lydia Davis, ed. Christopher Prendergast (2002), 84.

ACKNOWLEDGMENTS

For the very spirit of valour, special thanks to Linda Bell, Claudia Hamilton, John Hamilton, Paul and Katinka Hugenholtz, Caryl Phillips, Lauren Taylor, Meg Tyler, and Elise Wiarda.

This book would not exist, and would never have been finished, without the extraordinary support, encouragement, dedication, precision, and brilliance of Catherine Barnett, and the courage her company always brings.

Several friends read the manuscript in part or whole. For their illuminations, and for the quality of care in their attention, my deepest thanks to Rachel Eisendrath, Louise Glück, Jorie Graham, Robert Hass, Paul Keegan, Maureen McLane, Darryl Pinckney, Claudia Rankine, Christopher Ricks, John Ryle, and Rosanna Warren.

A simple listing of the following dear names does not capture my gratitude for their inestimable kindness to me during this late interregnum: Dr. James Aisenberg, Andrea Alaba, Peig van Amerongen, Alex Andriesse, Kevin Barr, Danielle Barry-Alicea, Christopher Baswell, Dr. Elizabeth Beautyman, Yasmin Begum, Angela Bernal, Susan Bernofsky, Sophie Cabot Black, Dr. Craig Blinderman, Daniel and Olivia Brush, Silla Brush, Valerie Zaloom Buccino, Rick Buckler, John Burghardt, Kathleen Campagnolo, Robert Chodo Campbell, Leslie Cawley, Ken Chen, Julie Crawford, Patricia Daily, Richard Deming, Thomas Dobson, Thomas Dodman, Dan Doniger, Ashley Fedor, James Fenton, Miranda Field, Jonathan Galassi, Regan Good, David and Lynn Grady, Hanna Graybill, Eliza Griswold, Sasha Guseynalieva, Andrew Hamilton, Emma Hamilton, James Hamilton, Nerissa Hamilton, Ross Hamilton, Langdon Hammer, Lisa Hollibaugh, Michiel and Madeline ter Horst, Claar Hugenholtz, Elise Hugenholtz, Finn Hugenholtz, Dr. David Ilson, Janna Israel, Dr. Tamara Jachimowicz, Doug

Jermyn, Nathalie Jones, Lycke Kagenaar, Tenzin Kelsang, LaShawn Keyser, Yun Kim, Michael Kirchberg, Rachel Klauber-Speiden, Suzanne Korff, Emily Kramer, Nancy Kuhl, Elisabeth Ladensen, Zoë Lamb, Sophie Lambrechtsen-ter Horst, Deborah Landau, Jane Lederer, John Lucas, Ula Lucas, Cybella Maffitt, Amy Martinez, Donna Masini, Fiona McCrae, Simone McCrorey, Katia Mota, Reshmi Mukherjee, Francis O'Neill, Koshin Paley-Ellison, Peter Platt, Paul and Marina Podolsky, Maya C. Popa, Laurie Postlewate, Jana Prikryl, Alice Quinn, Eliza Rathbone, Victoria Rosner, Peter Sacks, Haley Schoeck, Laetitia Schoofs, Jessica Schumacher, Kristyn Senzino, John Shackleton, Dr. Jyoti Sharma, Julie Sobel, David Stang, David Stephens, Dr. Vivian Strong, Timea Szell, Tom Thompson, Benedetta Tilli, Pier Mattia Tommasino, Jake Vogel, Matthew Vogel, Dorothée Volpini, Alexander van Wassenaer, Arent van Wassenaer, Diederik van Wassenaer, Geertruid van Wassenaer, Louise van Wassenaer, Just Wiarda, Dianne Wiest, Fiona Wilson, and Dr. Abraham Wu. And absent friends.

At Graywolf Press, the always superb guidance of Marisa Atkinson, Katie Dublinski, Carmen Giménez, and Jeff Shotts saw the book through production with patience and grace.

I am also most grateful to the Academy of American Poets, the American Academy of Arts and Letters, the Poetry Foundation, and the Zen Center for Contemplative Care for their support.

Selections from 'All Souls' appeared in *Harper's Magazine* (April 2023), the *New York Review of Books* (24 September 2020), and the *Yale Review* (Summer 2023).

'Museum Going' appeared in an earlier version as 'The Déjà-vu of His Sentences,' *Romanic Review* 111:3 (December 2020).

Saskia Hamilton is the author of three previous collections of poetry, *As for Dream*, *Divide These*, and *Corridor*. She is the editor of several volumes of poetry and letters, including *The Letters of Robert Lowell*, and is the co-editor of *Words in Air: The Complete Correspondence between Elizabeth Bishop and Robert Lowell*. Her edition of *The Dolphin Letters, 1970–1979: Elizabeth Hardwick, Robert Lowell, and Their Circle* received the Pegasus Award for Poetry Criticism from the Poetry Foundation and the Morton N. Cohen Award for a Distinguished Edition of Letters from the Modern Language Association. She is also the recipient of an Arts and Letters Award in Literature from the American Academy of Arts and Letters. She teaches at Barnard College.

The text of *All Souls* is set in Adobe Caslon Pro.
Book design and composition by Bookmobile Design & Digital
Publisher Services, Minneapolis, Minnesota.
Manufactured by Versa Press on acid-free,
30 percent postconsumer wastepaper.